# ONE WEEK

# SUCCESSION PLANNING DEMYSTIFIED

Other titles from IES:

**Free, Fair and Efficient: Open Internal Job Advertising**
Hirsh W, Pollard E, Tamkin P
Report 371, July 2000, ISBN: 1-85184-301-9

**Careers in Organisations: Issues for the Future**
Hirsh W, Jackson C,
Report 287, July 1995, ISBN: 1-85184-213-6

**Managing Careers in 2000 and Beyond**
Jackson C, Arnold J, Nicholson N, Watts A G
Report 304, June 1996, ISBN: 1-85184-230-6

**Strategies for Career Development: Promise, Practice and Pretence**
Hirsh W, Jackson C with Tamkin P, Kettley P, Jackson C
Report 305, June 1996, ISBN: 1-85184-231-4

**Towing the Line: Helping Managers to Manage People**
Bevan S, Hayday S
Report 254, April 1994, ISBN: 1-85184-177-6

A catalogue of these and over 100 other titles is available from IES, or on the IES Website, www.employment-studies.co.uk

*the* | **Institute**
*for* | **Employment**
| **Studies**

# Succession Planning
# Demystified

W Hirsh

Supported by the IES
Research
Club

Report 372

Published by:

THE INSTITUTE FOR EMPLOYMENT STUDIES
Mantell Building
Falmer
Brighton BN1 9RF
UK

Tel.   + 44 (0) 1273 686751
Fax   + 44 (0) 1273 690430

http://www.employment-studies.co.uk

**British Cataloguing-in-Publication Data**

A catalogue record for this publication is available from the British Library

ISBN 1-85184-302-7

**Printed and bound by Antony Rowe Ltd, Eastbourne**

# The Institute for Employment Studies

IES is an independent, international and apolitical centre of research and consultancy in human resource issues. It works closely with employers in the manufacturing, service and public sectors, government departments, agencies, professional and employee bodies, and foundations. For over 30 years the Institute has been a focus of knowledge and practical experience in employment and training policy, the operation of labour markets and human resource planning and development. IES is a not-for-profit organisation which has a multidisciplinary staff of over 50. IES expertise is available to all organisations through research, consultancy, publications and the Internet.

IES aims to help bring about sustainable improvements in employment policy and human resource management. IES achieves this by increasing the understanding and improving the practice of key decision makers in policy bodies and employing organisations.

## The IES Research Club

This report is the product of a study supported by the IES Research Club, through which a group of IES Corporate Members finance, and often participate in, applied research on employment issues. The members of the Club are:

Anglian Water
AstraZeneca
BOC
British Broadcasting Corporation
BT plc
Cabinet Office
Department of Trade & Industry
Department of the Environment,
  Transport and the Regions
Glaxo Wellcome plc
Halifax plc
HM Customs & Excise
HM Prison Service
Home Office

Inland Revenue
Lloyds TSB Group
Marks & Spencer plc
NHS Executive
Orange plc
Post Office
Rolls-Royce plc
Scottish Equitable
Scottish Executive
Shell UK Ltd
Smiths Industries
Standard Life
Unilever UK (Holdings) Ltd
Woolwich plc

## Acknowledgements

The author would like to thank the following people for their help and advice on this report: Peter Reilly, Alison Carter and Andy Davidson of IES; Helen Bartolome (Post Office); Nick Holley (M&G Ltd, Prudential); Geoff Williams (Unilever UK); Tony Ryan (BBC); Sherry H Stuckey (Glaxo-Wellcome); Sue Purves (AstraZeneca); Keith Brown (HSBC Bank plc); Stephen Dando (Guinness Limited); Les Slaytor, (Rolls-Royce plc).

# Contents

# Executive Summary

Succession planning is seen as a crucial process by most major employing organisations, but how well is it standing up to the uncertainty of business life today and the assumption that talented individuals will manage their own careers?

## What is succession planning?

Some of the confusion surrounding succession planning is due to people using the term in many different ways. Here we define **succession planning** to be a process by which one or more successors are identified for key posts (or groups of similar key posts), and career moves and/or development activities are planned for these successors. Successors may be fairly ready to do the job (short-term successors) or seen as having longer-term potential (long-term successors).

Succession planning therefore sits inside a very much wider set of resourcing and development processes which we might call **succession management**. This encompasses the management resourcing strategy, aggregate analysis of demand/supply (human resource planning and auditing), skills analysis, the job filling process, and management development (including graduate and high flyer programmes).

## What do organisations want from succession planning?

Organisations use succession planning to achieve a number of objectives including:

- **improved job filling** for key positions through broader candidate search, and faster decisions

- **active development of longer-term successors** through ensuring their careers progress, and engineering the range of work experiences they need for the future
- **auditing** the 'talent pool' of the organisation and thereby influencing resourcing and development strategies
- **fostering a corporate culture** through developing a group of people who are seen as a 'corporate resource' and who share key skills, experiences and values seen as important to the future of the organisation.

Of these, it is the active development of a strong 'talent pool' for the future which is now seen as the most important. Increasingly, this is also seen as vital to the attraction and retention of the 'best' people.

## Who does it cover?

The most common model for centralised, corporate succession planning is that it covers only the most senior jobs in the organisation (the top two or three tiers) plus short-term and longer-term successors for these posts. The latter group are often manifest as a corporate fast stream or high potential population who are being actively developed in mid-career through job moves across business streams, functions or geographical boundaries.

Many large organisations also adopt a 'devolved' model where the same processes and philosophy are applied to a much larger population (usually managerial and professional) but this process is managed by devolved business divisions, functions, sites or countries. It has to be said that few organisations successfully sustain the devolved model, usually because it is not really seen as a high priority and not adequately facilitated by HR.

## How are succession and development plans produced?

Succession plans normally cover both short- and longer-term successors for key posts, and development plans for these successors. Where a number of jobs are of similar type and need similar skills, it is preferable to identify a 'pool' of successors for this collection of posts.

**Typical activities** covered by succession planning include:

- identifying possible successors
- challenging and enriching succession plans through discussion of people and posts
- agreeing job (or job group) successors and development plans for individuals
- analysis of the gaps or surpluses revealed by the planning process
- review, *ie* checking the actual pattern of job filling and whether planned individual development has taken place.

The process is essentially one of **multiple dialogues.** Preliminary views are collected, usually from senior line managers, and then these views are tested and amended in a number of such dialogues: up the management line; with HR professionals; and in a committee of peers. The use of succession or development committees to challenge and agree plans is an important way of generating cross-boundary moves. They also help to ensure that the view taken by the organisation of an individual is based on objective evidence.

The level of secrecy in succession planning is gradually being reduced. All employees should understand that such a process exists and how it works. Those covered by the process should have an opportunity to make an input about their own career aspirations, preferences and constraints. They should also get feedback from the process in terms of how they are viewed by the organisation, their perceived development needs and the kinds of job moves for which they would be considered.

# Key linkages

Succession planning cannot stand alone. It is only of value if it is in tune with the business strategy and if its outputs (succession and career plans, and associated information) actually influence job filling and/or development. It therefore needs to link with:

- the **resourcing policy** for senior posts and broad brush **human resource planning,** *eg* the mix of internal development and external recruitment; the mix between generalist and functional career paths; the rough demand for successors of varied types over various timeframes

- strategies for **skill development** of those skills which will be needed over the coming years

- the **job filling** process, which needs to use succession planning information when a senior or key vacancy arises or when there is an opportunity to make a developmental move for someone. Organisations make this link in different ways. Succession plans can be used directly to make appointments, although this is less common today. More often, the plans and database searches feed into a shortlist which may also be augmented through open internal job advertising.

- **individual development plans** for those identified as part of the 'talent pool'. These are part of the succession process and should lead to both job experience (*eg* job moves, projects, secondments *etc.*) and skill training/coaching.

- **assessment processes**, which need to feed information into succession plans, for example from appraisal. This is part of the move to base judgements of potential on evidence against skill criteria needed for the job. It is important these cover job specific and functional skills as well as generic leadership competencies. Individuals need to be aware which sources of assessment information might be used in this way.

# A learning process which needs HR support

Modern succession planning is a learning process for all involved. Senior executives have to learn what kind of process will work best in their own business, given its unique structure and resourcing issues. They also need to learn how to hold these rather difficult discussions about the strengths and weaknesses of their people and how to best support their career development. The succession planning process therefore usually evolves over time as structures and needs change and executives get better at doing it.

The CEO has a critical role in giving priority to succession and in insisting on high quality, objective debate and follow-through. The HR function has an equally critical role in supporting the line. This is done in a number of ways, including process design and facilitation; challenging judgements and plans; broking crucial cross-boundary career moves; advice to those doing the planning; career counselling for individuals; and information support.

The information support role these days usually involves holding summary plans and supporting data on computerised databases. These databases should be kept as simple as possible but the information they contain should be continuously updated. This data becomes a valuable resource in its own right, especially for checking that developmental actions are followed up and in searching for internal candidates when vacancies arise.

# A changing process for changing times

Succession planning has come a long way from a process based on just putting names in boxes on organisation charts. Its main adaptations to changing needs are summarised below:

- Strong emphasis on using succession planning as a process for pro-actively developing 'talent', and therefore an emphasis on engineering developmental work experiences.

- Planning for 'pools' of jobs where possible, not just for individual posts.

- A more devolved model, with only very senior roles and small 'high potential' populations planned for at the corporate centre.

- Acceptance of the need for a more diverse senior management group, with functional strength as well as general management skills.

- Consideration of future skill needs as well as current skills (linked, but not restricted to, competence frameworks).

- More objective information on the performance, skills and potential of individuals, *ie* a meritocratic philosophy.

- A collective management process for identifying successors and taking responsibility for their development.

- More involvement of the individual and a gradual shift towards a more open approach. This includes adapting succession to take account of increasingly open internal job advertising.

- Less emphasis on 'the plan' but more on the dialogue and the valuable database which is built through the process and which can be used in a variety of ways (*eg* candidate search, during reorganisations *etc.*)

- Line ownership, often led by the CEO, with active facilitation and support from HR.

# Is it worth the effort?

Many writers have suggested that succession planning is too detailed a process to be appropriate in today's volatile environment. It is true that it still faces many tensions and challenges including the need to be flexible; to take on board that people make their own career decisions; and the need to increase the diversity of the talent pool, and especially to ensure that the talents of women and ethnic minorities are properly developed.

Organisations have found that, although management training goes some way to developing future leaders, it does not deliver the range of experience they require for future leadership roles. Succession planning is the only process we have which helps the organisation to deliver tailored, pro-active career development for its most talented individuals and align this with business needs. Most large organisations have concluded that modern succession planning is a crucial part of their HR strategy.

# 1. Introduction

## 1.1 Who is this report for?

Two types of people tend to ask the Institute of Employment Studies (IES) about succession planning. The first group are students of HR or practitioners who wish to broaden their understanding of HRM by getting to grips with what they see as one of its darker corners. The second group have a more urgent and alarming task. They have just been asked to write a Board Paper recommending an approach to succession planning and citing 'best practice' trends. They may even have just taken over direct responsibility for succession planning. This feels good because it is a somewhat prestigious task. It feels bad because they don't know where to start.

This report is an attempt to offer practical assistance to these two groups of people. It is not a detailed 'how to do it' guide but a practical overview of what is in reality a complex and wide-ranging subject. Its central mission is to demystify an HR process which is often shrouded in secrecy. The kind of succession planning described here is that typical of large employing organisations in the UK and international companies. Small and family businesses may find some of the ideas useful but will wish to adapt the process to their own needs and constraints.

This report is not primarily written for 'old hands' at succession planning, but it is hoped they may enjoy both agreeing and disagreeing with the views of the author and using it is a stimulus to further debate.

The report is a personal perspective which has grown out of numerous experiences of trying to help organisations establish or improve their succession planning processes over many years. It also builds on recent published research and dialogues at conferences and workshops.

## 1.2 What does the report cover?

The report attempts to answer some of the most commonly asked questions about succession planning:

- What is succession planning and what is it for?
- What do succession plans contain and how are they arrived at?
- How does succession planning link with business strategy and adjust to organisational change?
- How does succession planning link with other HR processes?
- How are succession plans used in job filling and in employee development?
- Does it make sense to plan when individuals manage their own careers?
- What kind of resources and support are needed to establish and maintain succession planning?
- Is it worth the effort?

Chapter 2 examines the nature and purposes of succession planning, and some of the arguments for and against formal succession planning.

Chapter 3 looks at the content of succession plans and how they are produced.

Chapter 4 looks at several ways in which succession planning can be more strongly linked to business and HR strategy.

Chapter 5 concentrates on four important linkages between succession planning and its inputs and outputs: assessment; job filling; development; and how the individual can both make inputs to the process and get feedback from it.

Chapter 6 looks at the resources needed to support the succession planning process.

Chapter 7 presents some general conclusions about whether succession planning is worth the time and trouble.

The key points of the report are summarised in the form of a list of practical tips in Chapter 8.

# 2. Defining Succession Planning and its Purposes

In this chapter we look at the basic ideas behind succession planning, and what organisations might hope to get out of it. We also explore the arguments for and against formal succession planning in a rapidly changing world.

## 2.1 Finding successors and getting them ready

The two basic ideas behind succession planning are simple and natural. The first idea is that of finding a successor to someone carrying out an important task or job so that the task can continue even if that person should leave the organisation or change job. The second idea is that of development. What does the successor (or several possible successors) need to be learning now to get them ready to take over when the time comes?

Large and small organisations have always had to grapple with issues of succession. Sometimes they have waited until the crisis is upon them to find a successor. Sometimes they have tried to prepare successors in advance so that a crisis is avoided. Succession *planning* is a systematic attempt to address the basic succession issue.

The antecedents of modern succession planning certainly go back at least 50 years in major employing organisations in the UK and US. Approaches developed considerably during the 1960s and early 1970s when large organisations were expanding and managers tended to stick with the same employer. Quite elaborate forms of succession planning evolved in both public and private sector organisations. Such plans were mainly aimed at identifying replacements for specific post-holders when they retired. Job moves were sometimes planned several steps ahead for individuals to prepare them for key roles. Organisations like the Civil Service and ICI ran computer simulations of how chains of jobs could be filled when a senior person left. International organisations (especially banks and oil companies) used succession plans to schedule the overseas postings of expatriates.

As we will see later, this rigid, secret and very detailed approach to succession planning (which we might call 'traditional') is quite a long way from contemporary practice. In particular, succession planning no longer assumes a static organisation, or that retirement will be the only cause of a chain of vacancies. As people move around more and jobs are often restructured, 'new style' succession planning has become a much more flexible management process. It is less elaborate and also less secretive. However, the age-old notions of identifying successors and planning their development still lie at its heart.

## 2.2 Defining succession planning and where it fits

Before we go any further we need to be slightly clearer about our definitions. Some people use the term 'succession planning' very broadly indeed and some much more narrowly. In this report we will use the term 'succession planning' to cover a fairly narrow and well defined set of activities, and the term 'succession management' to cover the much broader set of processes within which it sits.

**Succession planning** is taken here to be a process by which one or more successors are identified for key posts (or groups of similar posts), and career moves and/or development activities are planned for these successors. Successors may be fairly ready to do the job (short-term successors) or seen as having longer-term potential (long-term successors).

**Typical activities covered by succession planning include:**

- identifying possible successors
- challenging and enriching succession plans through discussion of people and posts
- agreeing job (or job group) successors and development plans for individuals

- analysis of the gaps or surpluses revealed by the planning process
- review, *ie* checking the actual pattern of job filling and whether planned individual development has taken place.

Succession planning is therefore an information generating process. Succession planning is only of value if its outputs (succession and career plans, and associated information) actually influence job filling and/or development by linking with other personnel processes.

Succession planning therefore sits inside a very much wider set of resourcing and development processes which we will call succession management.

**Succession management** encompasses the management resourcing strategy, aggregate analysis of demand/supply (human resource planning and auditing), skills analysis, the job filling process itself, and management development (including graduate and high flyer programmes). Figure 2.1 shows what succession planning covers and some of its linkages with other HR processes.

**Figure 2.1: Succession planning and its links with other HR processes**

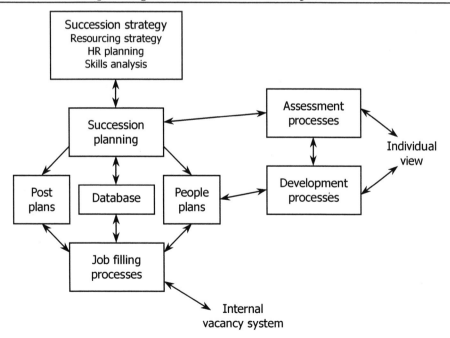

*Source: IES*

As the processes for dealing with employee development and assessment become more diverse, succession planning can become the process which integrates the career and development plans for an individual. As job filling processes change (*eg* through open advertisement) we need a clear view of how succession plans relate to job filling.

### Succession for which posts?

Although the concept of succession can, in theory, be applied to any kinds of posts, it tends to be applied most often to ensuring succession for the *top few layers* of the organisation. This form of succession planning is therefore a centralised, corporate activity.

As we will see in Chapter 3, succession planning can also be conducted on a *devolved* or local basis (*eg* for a department or an area or a function). In such cases, lower levels in the organisation are also likely to be included. Local plans can be co-ordinated and integrated in a way which links local and corporate succession.

## 2.3 Four objectives and some spin-offs

One of the reasons succession planning can seem elusive, is that it serves a number of different purposes in employing organisations.

Two objectives of succession planning are very tangible and relate back to its two core preoccupations:

1.  **Improving job filling** through broader candidate search, and faster decisions.

2.  **Active development** of longer term successors through ensuring their careers progress, and engineering the range of work experiences they need for the future.

'It is important to Unilever to identify and develop its future business leaders. A formal succession management process is designed to avoid "being in the right place at the right time" being the principal appointment mechanism. It is particularly important for managing the development of our highest potential managers.'

*Geoff Williams, Unilever UK* 99

To these two objectives we can add two more which are slightly less tangible:

3. **Audit and influencing wider succession management.** Many organisations see succession planning as a way of assessing or 'auditing' the 'talent' in the organisation. Are there enough successors for the different kinds of job roles? Are they good enough and do they have the right skills/attributes for the future? Are successors in the part of the business which most needs them? Is there a strong supply of people coming through who can take key roles in the longer term? Answering such questions should identify broader issues in senior management resourcing, deployment and development.

4. **Fostering a corporate culture.** Organisations often wish to see their most senior and high potential staff as a 'corporate resource'. By this they mean they should have the ability to deploy these people widely across the corporation, wherever their talents are most useful. In order to achieve this effectively, those individuals have to share some values and accepted modes of behaviour. Inculcating these values is part of the developmental objective of succession planning. Those making appointments (especially the Board) have to buy in to the notion of 'corporate resource' and not hang onto their own people. The succession process forces them to act more collectively.

Hall (1986) recognised these different purposes a long time ago and identified an evolution in succession, leading from a simple focus on filling a single post towards the broader and longer-term concerns.

In addition to these several purposes for succession planning, it has some 'spin offs' which are of potential value. They include:

- **Data on key posts and key people** pulled into one place or at least one format. This data (typically including details of current job holders, their career history and the skill requirements of jobs) is needed to support succession dialogues, but becomes an important resource in its own right.

- **Enhancing the people skills of executives.** We think of succession as delivering skill development to the identified successors. One of its potential benefits, however, lies in the development of those *doing* the planning not just those at the receiving end of it.

# 2.4 For and against succession planning

It is a curiosity of succession planning that it is simultaneously seen as a crucial process and as a most dubious one. Many of the world's most influential companies regard succession planning as crucial. Even those organisations which start out with a strong emphasis on flexibility and self-managed careers (like Sun Microsystems) reach a point in their development where corporate succession planning is seen as necessary. However, many management writers (Mayo, 1991; Liebman, 1996; Arnold, 1997; Holbeche, 1998) see succession planning (sometimes prefixed by the term 'conventional' or 'traditional') as a process past its sell-by date.

This difference of view may be more apparent than real. Writers critical of succession planning still seem to have in mind its 'traditional' manifestation: a secretive process of writing names of successors in the boxes of organisation charts and little more. Companies committed to succession planning — including several whose comments appear in this report — have in mind a 'new style' succession process which has evolved to meet contemporary challenges in ways this report attempts to highlight.

Before we look at the nuts and bolts of succession planning, it may help to list some of the arguments for and against it in the contemporary context. The criticisms of succession planning act as a useful checklist to see how well modern practices are dealing with the real challenges faced by succession today.

## 2.4.1 Against succession planning

- The desire to fill at least some senior jobs from outside the organisation. Is it an old fashioned idea that major employers will 'grow their own' talent?
- The difficulty of being sure what jobs there will be in even a few years' time and what skills will be most important.
- Successors identified by today's senior managers will be their own clones — an extension of the 'old boy network'.
- Identified successors may not choose to stay and may not accept the jobs you have planned for them.
- Most HR decisions are managed locally in devolved structures. Centralised, corporate succession planning cuts across the

responsibility local line managers have been given to deal with resourcing and employee development.

- A more fluid notion of 'career' and acceptance that individuals should manage their own careers, seem at odds with corporately planned careers.

## 2.4.2 For succession planning

- The need to be able to shortlist quickly for important job vacancies and to make good quality senior appointments. This requires information on the full range of strong internal candidates in order to have the best choice from which to select.

- The need to know the 'stock of talent' in the organisation in order to manage change (eg mergers, delayering) and face an uncertain future with confidence.

- Growth of individualised development attention for the best employees and a desire to broaden their experience in early and mid career. The need to focus such development on the skills and experiences most critical to the business.

- The need to offer tailored and varied career and development experiences in order to attract and retain the best employees.

- Continued interest in strong corporate cultures and how shared skills and experiences can reinforce this.

- It is irresponsible and dangerous to leave the future supply of leaders to chance. Without something like succession planning, the organisation is abnegating influence over its own future resources.

These kinds of outcomes demand a regular, systematic review of high potential employees and how they are being developed.

Most of the items on both the 'for' and 'against' lists, as summarised in Figure 2.2, apply in most organisations. So the real question is whether some form of succession planning can address the obvious needs while taking account of the difficulties inevitable in a turbulent and difficult environment.

**Figure 2.2: Summary of arguments for and against succession planning**

| For | Against |
|-----|---------|
| Effective shortlisting and best choice of internal candidates | Increasing external recruitment |
| Information on the 'talent pool' helps to manage unforeseen change | Impossible to forecast future manpower demand |
| Tailored career development for high potential individuals | Tendency to 'cloning' and 'old boy network' |
| Attraction and retention of 'the best' | Identified successors may leave |
| 'Corporate glue' and cross-boundary moves | Resourcing has been devolved to line managers in business units |
| Irresponsible to adopt a 'laissez faire' attitude to future business leaders | Individuals should be managing their own careers |

*Source: IES*

The Institute for Employment Studies

# 3. Succession Planning — the Mechanics

So now we have looked at the context in which succession planning sits, it is helpful to consider what goes into a succession plan and how such plans are arrived at.

For those who want more detail than is given here, some illustrations from the literature are given in the Appendix. A fairly full bibliography is also to be found at the back of this report including further reading relevant to the UK (Mayo, 1991; Hirsh, 1990; Wallum, 1993; IRS, 1997; Hirsh 1998) and the US (Eastman, 1995; Hall, 1986; Liebman, 1996). Several of these publications give detailed descriptions of succession planning practices.

## 3.1 Scope: what posts and which people?

One of the early practical decisions concerns the target group for succession planning, in other words which jobs the organisation will deal with in the succession process. There are a number of different populations which succession planning can cover, some of which are illustrated in Figure 3.1.

**Key posts** is a natural start point, but begs the question of what posts are 'key'. In a very small organisation nearly all jobs may be 'key' to continued production or service delivery. In larger organisations, defining key jobs has proved very difficult and most organisations have moved towards scoping succession planning by broad level of job.

**Top jobs:** In the US there is a vast literature about CEO succession, and the term succession planning there often seems to

**Figure 3.1: Which posts and which people?**

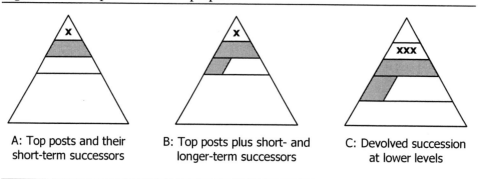

A: Top posts and their short-term successors

B: Top posts plus short- and longer-term successors

C: Devolved succession at lower levels

*Source: IES*

imply succession to the most important job in the organisation. In the UK, the term 'succession planning' usually implies a process for examining a range of senior jobs, not just the CEO. This group often aligns with jobs where the contract is specifically 'corporate' and where the appointment is made by the Chairman or the Board.

As shown in example A in Figure 3.1, a focus on 'top jobs' will lead to succession planning which covers the 'top jobs' (shown with an 'X') plus those in the organisational layer below (shaded in the diagram) who might be short-term successors for the top jobs.

**High potential people.** Example B in the diagram shows a common extension of this population to include not just short-term successors to the top jobs, but also longer-term successors. The shaded vertical 'slice' in model B represents a group of identified high potential staff (often also called a fast track) who will be included in the succession process as a means of managing their career and skill development in a pro-active way. Such 'high potential staff' are often in mid-career, typically in their thirties.

**Devolved succession planning,** as shown in example C on the diagram, can operate through local unit or functional managers simply deciding to be pro-active about the development of successors for the jobs within their own control. Some large organisations seek to use devolved succession planning in a more integrated way to cover the bulk of the professional and managerial workforce. Each unit or function carries out a compatible succession planning process for its own jobs and filters this information up into the levels above. So although only

The Institute for Employment Studies

the top few levels are considered in detail by the corporate centre, in effect a corporate-wide process has been created for a much larger population.

> We are learning to operate with devolved business structures which follow a Corporate template and a strong Corporate identity, values and behaviours.
>
> *Les Slaytor, Rolls-Royce plc* 🥂

So before we get into the detail of doing succession planning we need to be clear about:

- for which posts, or job groups we are going to identify successors
- which groups of employees are going to have their individual career (and possibly development) plans discussed by the succession planning process
- which managers in the organisation will be responsible for the succession process, *ie* the organisational location(s) involved.

These questions which define the scope of the succession planning process should relate to the resourcing strategy of the organisation (see Section 4.1) and the degree of devolution of responsibility for succession management.

It is crucial that the scope of succession planning should be manageable. It is far better to conduct good quality process which has real practical impact on a small population, than to deal half-heartedly with a much larger population.

Over the past ten years, the populations covered by succession planning at the corporate centre have been reducing. In an IES study conducted roughly ten years ago (Hirsh, 1990) the corporate centres of very large organisations were planning in detail for several hundred jobs and their successors — anything up to 700 or 800 people in total. Those same corporate centres today are mostly looking at a maximum of 200 or so jobs (very often dramatically less) and about half the numbers of people they would have attempted to cover ten years ago. This reduction in scale of centralised activity reflects the more devolved nature of HR in most large organisations and the impact of 'downsizing' and 'delayering.' The smaller scale of corporate succession planning may also reflect the practical upper limit of the numbers of people whose careers can be actively managed within one process.

A common pattern in the UK is that corporate succession covers the top two or three layers in the organisation (*eg* main and divisional boards and their direct reports) plus short- and longer-term successors for these posts. The organisation may also aspire to cover a much larger population through the devolved approach, but there is much variation in whether this is a vague hope or a process with clear design and serious commitment.

## 3.2 The contents of post and people plans

Let us assume for the moment that the succession planning process is fairly conventional in looking at particular jobs. Many organisations still do this, although they may also look at groups of jobs and skills (as we will see in the next section).

For all the mystique, the contents of succession plans are very simple and similar across organisations. Both post and person plans are commonly produced. They combine background information on the post or person with intentions about succession, as shown in Figure 3.2.

The post or position information is designed to record the kind of job it is and when it may need filling (if known). It is important to have simple and informative ways of classifying jobs. Key parameters for jobs tend to be:

- level as described by grade, job evaluation points or salary range
- organisational location *eg* business division, reporting line
- geographical location: country, region , area, site
- function, *eg* production, finance, personnel, IT, commercial, general management *etc.*
- role — less often used but very useful, *eg* operational management, strategic management, planning, expert adviser, project manager *etc.*

If such features of jobs are coded in a consistent fashion then the value of succession plans for searching for candidates is vastly enhanced.

Some organisations still identify 'emergency' successors (*ie* people who can take over in a crisis), although this is not usually a major focus of succession planning. A frequent distinction is between 'short-term' and 'longer-term' successors. A short-term

**Figure 3.2: Typical contents of succession plans**

| Post Plan | Person Plan |
|---|---|
| Position code/identifier | Personal ID |
| Job Title | Personal Details: Age, gender, ethnicity, family (if relevant) |
| Level, organisational and geographic location, function, role | Current job and characteristics *or link to job record* |
| Current job holder | Job History: Length of service, previous posts (by location, function, level) |
| Key characteristics of job holder: Age, length of service, grade, salary *etc. or link to person's record* | Assessments: Performance, potential, 360° feedback, strengths, weaknesses *etc.* |
| Status of position: Vacant, frozen, stable, date of planned change *etc.* | Qualifications/training (where relevant) |
| | Readiness for move as viewed by organisation |
| | Interests/aspirations of individual; PDP, experiences or job sought, mobility |
| **Successors *for post or type of post*:** | **Career Plan:** |
| Emergency | Short-term job options or job types |
| Short-term | Longer-term job options/direction |
| Longer-term | **Development needs and plans *eg courses, activities*** |

*Source: IES*

successor is usually just one job move away from the identified role, although they may still need some time to become fully ready for it. A longer-term successor is often someone who is two or three job steps away from the identified role, or about five years or so in terms of timescale. Although some organisations may identify 'high potential' employees very early in career, more these days look for potential for the highest levels once people are already in a substantial middle management role. Such people may well feature on succession plans as longer-term successors.

Person plans are more variable than post plans. In the past, person plans quite often included 'final destination' and/or a detailed career path mapped out several jobs ahead. Person plans are now more likely to focus on a range of jobs for which the person would be suitable in the short-term (plus a timescale for this) and also some indication of their longer-term potential and career direction and development needs.

## 3.3 Planning for posts, pools or skills?

As we have seen in Section 2.4, one of the arguments against succession planning is that posts are now too volatile to plan for, and so planning for specific positions may not be helpful.

One response to this issue is to go on planning for individual posts on the grounds that short-term succession still needs to be managed. In addition, many companies have found that it is only when an individual is considered against a particular post that their real strengths and weaknesses are properly discussed.

Some critics of succession planning argue that it is better to plan for skills than to plan for posts. Although this sounds plausible, it doesn't deliver the same dialogue as a post- or role-based one. Many large organisations have already defined key management skills (often called competencies) and these would feature in the skill assessments for individuals. However, succession also needs to consider functional skills (*eg* finance), situational skills (*eg* ability to turn round part of the business), team fit and so on. IES research on planning in terms of skills (Hirsh and Reilly, 1998) found that organisations were poor at defining their future skill needs and even poorer at measuring how much of a skill was in the current workforce.

A recent survey of succession practices among major employers (Hirsh, 1998) found that most of those practising succession planning still identified short-term successors for specific posts, although only a minority sought to identify specific posts for long-term successors.

A practical mid-ground is offered by the notion of planning for some groups or 'pools' of posts, or for typical job roles, either in addition to, or instead of, planning for each specific post.

For example, if a retail or service organisation is spread around the country, there may be a number of Area or Regional General Managers. Although circumstances will vary from place to place, many of the same skills will be needed in each of these positions and the same pool of successors may be relevant to most of the posts. It therefore makes sense to develop successors for this **pool** of posts of similar type and fine tune the best candidates when specific vacancies arise.

Another way of looking at this is to classify posts by **role** and possibly also by **function** and **level**. For example, the finance function may have a number of planning type jobs at senior management level, so 'senior financial planning' could be an appropriate pool to plan for and might require different skills from, say, 'operational finance' roles at the same level.

The Post Office has adopted this approach in order to plan better for clusters of similar senior roles across a diverse business. It differentiates between specialist roles and unit management roles. It also distinguishes the main functions of the business, *eg* service delivery, call centres, marketing, business support (IT, HR, finance). So a typical pool might be potential MDs of service delivery units. This framework was initially based on an analysis of the content of senior jobs, but has since evolved in response to its use and a major reorganisation.

If posts can be viewed in this way, then there will be a pattern of generic skills which is often common for types of role (*eg* planning roles often require analytical ability and strategic thinking; operational roles require greater people leadership ability). The function of a job role often determines the type of specific knowledge or skills required (*eg* knowledge of markets, technology, systems *etc.*).

There are dangers in assuming that people will always stay within the same function and one of the main purposes of succession planning is to engineer cross-functional moves for selected individuals. However, information on the functional requirements of posts and the functional experience of individuals is needed to make judgements about which individuals need particular experience of other functions.

## 3.4 How plans are arrived at: the succession planning process

There are some choices about where the succession planning process starts.

One common start point is for each senior player (*eg* head of function or division) to be asked to identify:

1. one or more short-term successors for each of the posts in scope to the exercise

2. individuals within their areas seen as having high potential and/or being possible longer term successors for the posts in scope to the exercise.

They may also be asked to comment on a range of other related issues such as:

- general perceptions of the quality of available candidates for types of post
- ability to recruit externally
- impact of expected business changes on demand for numbers and types of people
- skill gaps between what the business needs, and the skills of the current population
- jobs which are hard to fill because they are unattractive
- individuals who need a cross-functional or cross-unit move.

In a devolved succession process, this initial information will be requested from managers at various levels and fed up through the line.

For the corporate population, the initial succession information is then often discussed with a senior HR manager (*eg* HR Director or Management Development Director). This allows for a degree of challenge before the information is shared with peers. Sometimes the Chief Executive or MD joins these individual meetings with heads of functions or divisions.

The next step is for this information to be collated and then debated within the senior peer group responsible for succession. At the top of the company this would normally be the Board. In a devolved process, a committee might be the management group of a site or unit or function.

Sometimes HR generate background data first. In the case of repeated rounds of succession planning, this data can include a summary of what was decided last time, allowing key players to check whether development actions were followed up. Background information can also include the demographic, gender and ethic mix of the workforce (important if diversity is a key issue) and wastage rates over the previous period.

The collective senior dialogue is used to reach a shared view of people and the needs of posts and to amend/endorse the succession and development plans. Candidates are often added from outside the business unit. Key cross-functional and cross-unit moves needed for development are agreed.

Although the process needs to be systematic, disciplined and objective, it is very important that it isn't mechanistic. It is fundamentally a process based on management judgement and managers' perceptions of which issues are important at any point in time.

'You need to bring science to succession planning — but it is more of an art than a science.'

*Keith Brown, HSBC* **99**

Some American companies are fabled to have vast charts pinned up on Boardroom walls and to go through every job ratifying a list of successors. More commonly, the senior debate will focus on jobs or types of jobs where there are perceived to be problems and on individuals needing cross-boundary moves.

After the dialogue has been completed, an overall report is often produced which highlights key issues as well as summarising plans for posts and people. HR often has a critical role in analysing the results of the succession planning process to highlight areas of strength and weakness in the talent pool. It is important to look for patterns within the overall picture and identify functions, divisions or locations where succession cover is relatively weak. This may indicate a need to redeploy some successors from one part of the business to another when such opportunities are available.

'You need to take various cuts at the succession information, geographically, functionally, by business stream etc. It is these subsets of the corporate perspective which give real insight into areas of strength or weakness.'

*Helen Bartolome, Post Office*                                         **99**

The whole succession process is often conducted as a 'cycle'. This combines continuous attention to agreed actions and updating information with periodic systematic reviews as described above. The full cycle is often annual, although it can be more or less frequent than this. One organisation used the process one year to concentrate mainly on succession for posts and the next year would start the discussion for each division by looking at the development plans for high potential individuals. This staved off boredom and also ensured that the developmental agenda got serious attention.

In between major reviews, it is important that the HR function keeps the plans up to date to reflect real job moves occurring.

Succession planning is sometimes part of a wider review of staffing or management development. This may have a variety of names: Human Resources Review, Business Review, Management Development Review *etc.* Being part of wider system has considerable advantages in term of links with business planning (see Section 4.2), but can make the succession review too cursory.

# 3.5 Succession planners do it in committees

Committees are a famously bad way of getting things done. In the case of succession planning, however, committees have proved an important improvement on the previous practice of each senior manager 'cooking up' their own succession plan with the collusion of someone from personnel.

The committee responsible for succession for the top of the organisation is often the Board or the key executive members of it. It is normally chaired by the CEO or MD with HR present in a facilitating role. It may call itself a Succession Committee or Management Development Committee. Sometimes the process is given a name, *eg* Management Development Review.

When such committees meet they need a clear and fairly simple **agenda**. This might include:

- review of progress made against actions agreed in the previous cycle

- key points arising from local reviews: problems areas (*eg* loss of key people); skill changes; jobs dangerously short of cover; planned key external recruitment — the big picture

- what to do about any problem jobs or job groups, including additional successors identified in other parts of the business

- key job moves planned for individuals, especially those across organisational or functional boundaries

- the health of the longer-term pipeline in the various functions or job groups and whether any of these individuals need critical moves or development activities.

A committee approach has a number of key advantages:

- Executives are more likely to prepare thoroughly and to have looked at assessment evidence if they have to justify their opinions on people in front of their peers and the CEO.

- These opinions are shared and argued out in a structured way. This can surface legitimate queries about people and allow a more rounded view of them to be reached.

- If one committee member says they are in agreement with a particular cross-boundary move for an individual, they are in effect making a public promise that they will give this move their support when the opportunity arises for it to happen. They have had their chance to query it and cannot easily then block it.

- Senior people love talking about individuals and hate talking about HR strategy. Through discussing a whole range of people and posts, senior teams see patterns in the management population and start a more focussed and practical debate on aspects of resourcing and development strategy.

- Reviewing previous succession plans as part of the process provides a check on whether developmental actions have been followed up. Again senior people are more likely to do this if they are going to have defend their action (or lack of it) at a meeting of their peers and in front of the CEO.

In addition to the Board discussing top level succession, functional committees may well review the functional populations across the corporation (*eg* in finance, personnel, commercial functions *etc.*).

In organisations operating a devolved succession approach, there may be quite complex networks of committees reviewing different levels and types of posts and people. For example, Rolls-Royce uses the term 'Development Cells' for the committees in such a structure. Because they are devolved, they can cover most of the professional workforce in a large company and develop a much broader population than corporate succession planning can alone.

Such sets of committees can be linked together through their membership. For example, if each factory manager in a manufacturing business looks at succession for their own post and their site team, this information can be brought to the next level up: a meeting of several factory managers with the MD of their business stream or division or country.

Although many organisations sustain regular corporate succession committees at the highest level, fewer sustain this integrated, devolved model. This is partly because it is much more complex, but also because it may not be adequately resourced at local level (see Section 6.3) or seriously demanded by the Board. Without strong interest from the corporate centre, operating units tend to adopt a rather short-term approach to resourcing and allow their succession planning to lapse.

## 3.6 Succession planning as dialogue and learning

Our first model of succession planning in Chapter 2, we pictured succession planning as a process linked with other, related processes of: appraisal, job filling, development *etc*. This approach tends to highlight the flow of information from one system to another.

Another useful way of looking at succession is as a whole mesh of conversations by which this information flow actually takes place.

In addition to the senior forums described above, several other kinds of dialogue are important, as shown on the diagram below.

They normally include:

● conversations up and down the line to identify high potential staff and reach a view of individuals' strengths and weaknesses from those who work closely with them

The Institute for Employment Studies

- discussions between individuals and their line managers, sharing assessment information and obtaining an understanding of the individual's aspirations and development needs

- discussions between the Personnel function and the line at various levels to challenge draft plans and to identify extra successors for jobs in other areas of the business

- discussions between Personnel and individuals to discuss their aspirations, preferences and constraints. Individuals often find it difficult to discuss these matters with their boss, especially if they want to a job move to another area

- feedback to individuals from the succession process, through the line or Personnel, to inform them in general terms about how they are perceived and their future career options.

Some of these conversations are planned and formal, for example between the HR director and divisional heads, or between the CEO and the Executive Committee. Most are one-to-one conversations and take place throughout the year: informing succession plans; before and after performance reviews; feeding back on plans; and when vacancies arise.

The dialogue process seems central to effective succession planning. Chambers *et al.* (1998) make this point in relation to the leadership team actively reviewing the current pool of talent through:

**Figure 3.3: Succession dialogues**

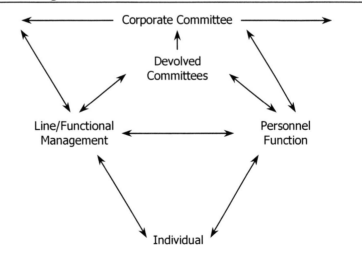

*Source: IES*

*'...regular discussions to review the performance of executives at every level. The backbone of a company's talent effort, these reviews must be candid, probing, and action-oriented, and link talent to strategy.'*

'It's not the process and the paperwork that matter, but the quality and frequency of the dialogue between all the key players.'

*Nick Holley, M&G Ltd (Prudential)*                                     99

Reaching a shared view of a person's skills and potential, demands dialogues which are challenging and probing but also objective and constructive. Managers need to try and put their personal prejudices to the back of their minds and focus on the recent evidence relevant to an individual which is brought to any discussion. It helps to agree criteria for the job against which successors will be considered.

It is through these discussions that succession planning also becomes a learning process for all those involved. This may be one reason why we see that the real impact of succession planning takes time to develop. Although we can design a theoretical succession process on paper very quickly, the implementation of this as a process involving real people takes a long time to mature. Many organisations give up on succession planning after a few months of finding it an uphill struggle. It might be better to expect it to take several years.

'Invariably senior managers value the time spent on what could be called 'succession coaching', ie being questioned, prompted and stretched on the possible future plans for their organisation and the capabilities of their people to help them to succeed.'

*Tony Ryan, BBC*                                     99

It takes an organisation of considerable maturity to manage such complex interactions, and the Figure 3.3 shows the pivotal role often played by the HR function in bridging between the different players involved.

# 4. Succession and HR Strategy

So far we have concentrated on how succession planning works. But how does it fit within the wider business and HR strategy? HR people often say they want an 'integrated' approach, but how can you achieve this in practice?

In this chapter we look at a number of ways in which succession planning can both build on and inform business and HR strategy. We will examine its links with executive resourcing strategies, human resource planning, the identification of future skill needs, and corporate culture. It also needs to integrate with other HR processes and may be helped by the fact that the executive team responsible for succession is already involved in all these aspects of the business.

## 4.1 The resourcing strategy for senior positions

Succession planning only makes sense if the organisation has a strategy of filling many of its senior roles from within. Major employers have come to realise that the quality of their management is perhaps the least replicable aspect of business excellence, and therefore a real lever for business advantage. If they recruit many of their top people they cannot easily sustain such an advantage. Most large employers do recruit some people at senior levels for specific skills and fresh attitudes and consider it important to do so. However, they do not wish to be forced to the open market as a result of an inadequate supply of talent within.

The dominant strategy is to try and identify some people with 'high potential' at an early enough career stage to ensure they have a broad enough range of work experience to prepare them

**Figure 4.1: Typical components of proactive senior management resourcing**

Selective external recruitment operates
alongside all these models

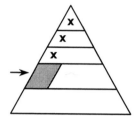

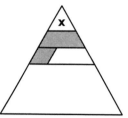

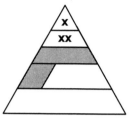

Managed early career
*eg* graduate entry scheme

Corporate succession and
high potential development

Devolved succession
extending further down

*Source: IES*

for strategic and general management roles. This approach is pursued both through graduate entry programmes (to bring in some high potential employees) and so called 'fast-track' or 'high flier' schemes (to focus high potential mid-career development). This strategy has obvious links with a succession planning approach which both identifies and agrees development of a high potential mid-career population.

> 'We want to grow our own, we like to ensure we have the very best people coming through, but we acknowledge that, occasionally, recruitment to fill key roles is an acceptable part of succession planning.'
>
> *Keith Brown, HSBC*                                                    **99**

Figure 4.1 shows these varied strategies. A managed early career route is a way of bringing in high potential people for the longer term. Such early career schemes, often graduate entry schemes, offer proactive development for several years (*eg* accountancy, Civil Service fast stream). Graduate schemes may be corporately managed or more devolved to business units or functions. Corporate schemes are often run by the same individual or department as manages senior succession. Even if they are not part of the succession planning process *per se*, the same processes of career and development planning are normally applied.

Corporate succession planning combined with a mid-career high potential or fast track scheme deals with those further into career who are seen as having potential for very senior roles. They probably feature as longer-term successors on the corporate succession plans.

The devolved approach, with succession planning at local, functional or divisional levels, fits with an HR strategy based on proactive development of a much broader raft of managers and professionals. It is most often found in organisations with a high proportion of professional or specialist staff.

Many organisations are practising all three of these strategies at the same time, and simultaneously selectively recruiting from outside at every level as well. It is a kind of 'belt and braces' approach to succession — mixing internal and external talent, fast track and slow burn development, and attending to varied career stages and levels.

## 4.2 Links with human resource planning

'You must first look at the "macro" — how many people, what skills and experiences, what fields and disciplines — before you look at the "micro" of who, where, when.'

*Keith Brown, HSBC*

In terms of numbers, succession planning seldom looks far ahead at how the size of the management population may need to change. Is succession planning really looking ahead at changing business needs, when it attempts to 'audit' management talent? The answer is that the identification of successors does not, in itself, constitute a serious audit of future supply. It tends to highlight current shortages and surpluses in terms of both numbers and skills. Broad human resource planning (HRP) should inform the succession process of changing demand resulting from changing business needs and structure.

We also need to be aware that the number and type of successors required does not only depend on changing demand but also on the likely rate of flow of people through the organisation. This in turn is influenced by the demography of the current population, retirement and early retirement policies, and trends in wastage rates at earlier career stages. HRP can reveal gaps whch are likely as a result of the interaction between current demography, future retirement and natural wastage. It can also help to establish how far ahead succession planning should attempt to look.

For some mysterious reason, organisations usually consider themselves well resourced if they can find three to five successors for each key post. In high wastage organisations, more than this number of successors will be needed. It is important to check that the identified talent pool does offer the organisation some choice in candidates and that the same successors haven't been put down for all the jobs!

If the organisation has goals for shifting the mix of its senior population (for example, as public sector organisations have for women and ethnic minorities), some simple HRP analysis is vital to knowing whether such goals are attainable.

Succession planning should also inform HRP. For example, an analysis of the talent pool by level, function, location *etc.* as described in Section 3.3 can highlight parts of the business which need a more thorough review of management resourcing and may require selective recruitment or intensive development.

## 4.3 Skills for the future

'The key challenge for succession planning isn't ensuring there is succession cover in the current structure. By the time the need arises the world will have changed. The real challenge is looking at succession cover for roles which don't even exist today but which will emerge as the organisation and its strategy evolve.'

*Nick Holley, M&G Ltd (Prudential)*                                          **99**

HRP needs to be qualitative as well as quantitative. It should influence the kinds of skills being developed for the future and also the range of experiences sought for successors. This is not as easy as it sounds. For example, those many UK organisations which are acquiring subsidiaries or partners abroad obviously need some more understanding of international issues, but what does this really mean? Should all high potential people have to work overseas, or can they get the same knowledge by working on multi-cultural project teams from their home country? Do they need languages? Which functions/levels in the organisation will be most affected by growing internationalisation? Is recruiting a few graduates from other countries another answer? Whichever solution is adopted, the organisation needs a clear analysis of the skills it is seeking to develop and how it will manage international job moves.

The common answer these days seems to be 'competencies' as though these magically attune succession to the organisation's future needs for leadership skills. One of the downsides of many competence frameworks is that they have not been derived with the future in mind, so they lag behind the skills which succession planning should be considering. They may also place too much emphasis on generic and personal skills at the expense of specialist and functional skills.

Fashions also come and go with regard to the kinds of senior managers organisations wish to develop. The 1980s was the decade of the General Manager — an all-seeing, all-knowing being who had experience of many functions (but may have been master of none). With the downsizing of the 1990s we have seen the return of the senior manager who is both a functional expert and a people leader. It seems to be the functional leadership positions (IT, Finance, Marketing and HR Directors) which have been difficult to resource. These people may be harder to grow than general managers.

The succession process at least needs to encourage discussion of new skill needs which are already emerging and how they might be further encouraged. Crystals balls are problematic, but skill changes are rarely rapid. They more often emerge over a period of several years. Looking at jobs which are hard to fill often gives clues as to skills which are already lacking. A current example might be leaders who can lead and implement very large and complex system changes (such as so often fail to deliver), or who can negotiate successful mergers or alliances (ditto).

Looking at the big changes in the structure and nature of business also gives us some broad clues. Chambers *et al.* (1998) pick on 'global acumen; multi-cultural fluency; technological literacy; entrepreneurial skills and the ability to manage increasingly delayered, disaggregated organizations'.

---

'Who predicted the impact that the internet and e-commerce would have, ten years ago, and if you did what did you do about it? However, I will predict one thing, that in ten years from now, we will not have foreseen 2010 correctly — so "nimbleness" has to be a key attribute.'

*Keith Brown, HSBC*　　　　　　　　　　　　　　　　　　　　　**99**

## 4.4 The business and management culture

It is very difficult to conceive of succession planning being useful in organisations which are:

1. so devolved they do not seek a corporate culture at all, or
2. extremely short-term in their business thinking, or
3. do not take the management of people very seriously.

Although the largest and most successful organisations are usually corporate, long-term and serious about management, this does not apply universally. Very new organisations tend not to have long-term pre-occupations, being more concerned with getting themselves established and surviving the perilous first few years.

Some sectors work by very separate teams focussing on specific aspects of the business. Some parts of the financial sector are still collections of baronies with teams flitting round the City from one to the next. Although some of the 'barons' look at succession within their own teams, such organisations find it very difficult to embed a shared, corporate approach to succession. This is partly because of the highly volatile labour market (and a resourcing strategy based largely on head-hunting) but also because the barons don't play ball with each other very easily (see Hirsh, 1998).

## 4.5 Linking succession to other HR processes

Integration with HR strategy also means that the succession process has explicit links with other HR policies, processes and frameworks. Some of the most important linkages are with the assessment process, the way jobs are filled, and the way pro-active development is delivered. These key linkages are explored further in the next chapter.

> Ask people to manage their careers and they will expect to have options and choices in the tools and techniques they use.
>
> *Les Slaytor, Rolls-Royce plc* **99**

The philosophy of succession also has to sit consistently alongside the wider HR philosophy of the organisation. This presents a challenge, as the 1990s saw widespread emphasis on self-managed careers. We explore this issue in Section 5.4 on how succession planning links with the individual employee.

## 4.6 Strategic linkage through the management team

Another way of thinking about the relationship between succession and business strategy is to recognise that the same people do both. This may after all be the most powerful way of making a real link. A Board which has been discussing a major overseas venture one week will, if reminded it is relevant, bear this in mind when considering their succession plans the next week. Once reminded, they can bring their understanding of the business issue to their consideration of future posts and people. It would be nice to think that a succession strategy can sometimes lead a business through an important change. Tichy (1996), presents a graphic and unusual account of how the selection and development of a pool of potential future leaders at Ameritech was part of the process of changing business strategy and how the successors took ownership of that change.

The recent McKinsey study of 'the war for talent' in corporate America (Chambers *et al.*, 1998) argues that if 'talent' comes first, business success will follow. They place rightful emphasis on the mindset with which executives approach the broad succession management agenda:

> 'You can win the war for talent but first you must elevate talent management to a burning corporate priority.'

HR practitioners can wait forever to work for executives who see talent management as passionately as this. Succession planning, although of itself a rather pedestrian concept, may just lead some executives towards a better understanding of how important talent management really is. It confronts them with real examples of where posts could be filled but for a lack of certain skills or lack of having retained some key players. Such deficits can leave important projects under-resourced or business developments delayed. If executives experience these real-life links between the development of key staff and their ability to move the business forward, they may start to see the link between succession and their real business agenda.

# 5. Integration of Succession: Key Inputs and Outputs

The overall model presented in Chapter 2 showed succession planning in its strategic context as we have just been exploring. It also showed a number a key linkages. These linkages answer the question about how we integrate succession planning with other HR practices.

It is through these linkages that succession planning rests on good quality assessments of people (Section 5.1) and actually influences job filling (Section 5.2) and employee development (Section 5.3). The links between succession planning and the individual employee are also crucial (Section 5.3).

A recent study in 40 organisations, by Andrews and Munroe (1999) found a weak link between succession planning and agreeing actions. The links in this chapter are some of those required for there to be a better carry-through from succession planning to some practical actions.

## 5.1 Succession and assessment

The most profound challenge posed by succession planning is that the organisation needs to be able to 'take of view' of someone, not just in relation to their current job performance, but also their potential for an uncertain future. And this has to be done by managers all over the organisation in a serious and fairly consistent way. The whole process will have little credibility if the assessment of individuals is seen to be too casually conducted or too partisan. This is where the criticisms of 'cloning' and 'old boy networks' come in.

In 'traditional' succession planning, the assessment of individuals as successors was either tacked onto the appraisal process (through a tick box system) or conducted quite separately through just asking line managers who they thought could fill various jobs. Now organisations have developed more rigorous and multiple forms of assessment, we need to be clear how these feed into succession plans.

In linking assessment to succession, the following points should be borne in mind:

- **Check the relevant skills are considered.** Define the kinds of skills which are most important for the role or group of roles in question. Each successor then needs to be looked at against these criteria. A backcloth may be provided by a generic framework of senior management or leadership competencies (*ie* behavioural descriptions of positive leadership styles and characteristics). But other job specific skills are also relevant and must be considered. Skills more important for the future should also be included. One very simple model is to consider three types of skill criteria: functional skills; people/leadership skills; and business/strategic skills.

- **Assessment based on evidence and serious debate.** A climate is needed in which assessment of individuals through appraisal is taken seriously and where evidence of aspects of performance is required to support judgements being made. The challenge process made possible by the dialogues and committees (as described in Chapter 3) is an important safeguard against senior managers just nominating people they like.

---

'One of the most constructive activities in the succession planning process is for managers to share, debate and test their views and observations on the potential of their people. Too often the process does not include this valuable learning.'

*Tony Ryan, BBC*                                    **99**

---

- **Using appraisal data.** Detailed appraisal information, often including feedback against some specified management competencies, should be looked at by those suggesting people as successors. The succession dialogue should also refer back to such inputs for evidence.

- **Additional sources of assessment data.** In addition to boss-subordinate appraisal, 360 degree feedback is increasingly used to augment the view of the line. In some companies (*eg* BP) where this form of review has been running for some time, it is a major input to succession planning.

- Another way of checking assessments is to get views from past as well as present line managers, although very old data should be treated with caution.

- Some organisations check their judgements with the use of assessment or development centres either at the gateway to senior management or to identify high potential people earlier in career.

- **Clarity about data sources used.** If such additional sources of assessment information feed into succession planning, this should be clearly explained to employees. This is especially important with forms of assessment (*eg* psychometrics, development centres, 360 degree feedback) which are often introduced to help individuals with their own personal development. It should be made clear whether such information will feed into succession planning or whether it remains the private property of the individual.

- **Performance and potential.** People seen as 'high potential' should also have achieved high performance in their current jobs. One company uses the phrase 'potential equals performance plus' as a salutary reminder that high potential individuals have to continue to prove their worth. However, not all good performers will have high potential. It is important that the line have a shared view of 'potential' when they are asked to identify people who have it! Very abstract models based on ultimate destination grades (*eg* Board level potential) are extremely difficult to use consistently. It may be more realistic to ask for managers to identify people in the top ten per cent of performers or those who might be able to do a job two levels above their present job. At least these definitions are a bit more comprehensible to the average line manager.

Attention to these issues has improved assessment in relation to succession, but some approaches can become dysfunctional if taken to extreme. The rigid profiling and scoring of individuals against jobs may sell software packages but does not provide a good holistic overview of a person. Likewise, using leadership competence frameworks in a very restrictive way may omit other vital skill requirements or strengths of the person which are 'not on the list'. Assessment centres can easily favour some types of staff more than others. For example, they can disadvantage technical people in relation to those coming from commercial or operational functions. This is because business strategy exercises favour those who have been working in commercial areas and specialists may have also had less practice at certain types of communication and influencing.

The issue of 'ambition' is also a tricky one. Organisations need people with a degree of ambition to fill senior roles, but ambition and talent are not the same thing. Some of the best people are not very ambitious. Some of the most ambitious people may lack key skills and may be so busy 'managing upwards' that they give little attention to 'managing downwards.' One of the merits of 360 feedback is it is more likely to reveal whether people who are delivering good results are doing so at the expense of those around them. Organisations need to realise that the promotion of people who do not manifest key organisational values (*eg* supporting and developing their own subordinates; respect for the individual; teamworking) produces deep cynicism among the staff. Assessment processes need to check carefully for these value-sensitive behaviours.

Even improved assessment practices have not solved the problem of lack of diversity at senior levels. There are persistent problems with recognising 'high potential' in groups not previously represented at very senior levels, especially women. Executives need to be aware of this problem and also of the very subtle forms of discrimination based on behavioural differences between cultures and genders. They also need to test the assumptions they make about other people's level of ambition. 360 degree assessment processes may in time help to highlight the potential of women (Fletcher, 1999). Women and ethnic minorities also need encouragement to apply for more senior roles, and organisations need to make sure that mid-career development for high potential people is compatible with family life.

## 5.2 Succession and job filling

We have looked at a crucial input to succession planning: assessment information. We now turn to two crucial outputs: job filling and development.

Job filling processes are many and varied. They can be closed or open, formal or informal, objective or subjective. They can involve the personnel function intimately or not at all. If we do not influence the appointment process, directly or indirectly, we cannot improve succession management.

So how does the succession process link with the way senior roles are filled?

There are broadly three models we see in operation:

- Succession plans generate some candidates, often using a database trawl in addition to those specifically identified as successors for that job role. A range of possible candidates is thereby identified. These candidates can be dropped straight onto a short-list, although someone needs to check the individual is interested in the job! Other candidates may also be suggested by managers or be shortlisted through an open advertisement process. All shortlisted candidates would then go through a selection process, most often an interview.

- In open internal job markets, the succession planning system may be used to advise certain candidates to apply. Their applications then go in with other people who have seen the post advertised and choose to apply. Some organisations flag in the internal job ad that they have a 'preferred candidate' for the post (Hirsh, Pollard and Tamkin, 2000). Employees see this as an open way of dealing with the fact that succession planning does give planned candidates a special status in the selection process.

- Some organisations fill jobs directly from the succession plan without going through any form of internal advertising. This is still common practice for the very highest levels of the organisation, but is becoming less common lower down (Hirsh, Pollard and Tamkin, 2000).

In addition, key roles or ones which might be hard to fill may be advertised externally in parallel with an internal process. In the public sector, all posts above a certain level are commonly advertised nationally in the press.

Recent IES research into how jobs are filled (Hirsh, Pollard and Tamkin, 2000) found that employees by and large accept the corporate rationale for succession planning and high potential schemes as one way of highlighting possible candidates for jobs. What they do not accept is an organisation being secretive about the nature of the process, or having jobs advertised when they really have already been filled.

# 5.3 Succession and development

The pro-active development of high potential people is the most important objective of succession planning today. This focuses mainly on longer-term successors, although some short-term development for those nearer the top of the business may also be included. So how does succession help to identify development needs, and how are these needs addressed?

## 5.3.1 Defining desirable experiences and skills

Succession planning looks at skills (as do many other HR processes) but perhaps its real strength from a development perspective lies in trying to link skill development with specific career experiences, past and future.

In 'traditional' succession planning, career experience was rather a sheep dip, attempting to give aspiring general managers a whole range of experiences designed to broaden their skills. In the 1980s a typical list might have been: unit management roles, head office/planning roles, overseas experience (in international companies), plus experience of several functions.

Some of the sheep dip approach still remains, as does the fundamental objective of broadening the individual's skill base. However there are more and more things we would like executives to have experienced.

Examples from the ever-lengthening list might now include:

- operational and strategic roles (often 'field' and Head Office)
- critical support functions: Finance, HR but increasingly IS, logistics, quality *etc*
- managing people of different kinds (*eg* leading large workforces but also managing teams of professionals)
- managing key customers
- working on wider societal issues, *eg* with governments, community groups, education, environmental issues *etc*
- dealing with the media
- working with different national cultures
- managing major change, including technological change, mergers and alliances

- leading major projects
- managing start-ups and run-downs.

It certainly helps if there are just a few things seen as important for virtually every senior person (*eg* strategy formulation experience; leading some significant change; people leadership) and then others (*eg* direct international experience; technology) which may apply only to some roles or functions.

Part of the job of the succession planning process is to prioritise specific types of experience which will develop an individual's skills in an appropriate way.

## 5.3.2 Tailored experiences for individuals

The delivery of a broader range of work experience relevant to the needs of the business (as above) but tailored to the individual's skill set and aspirations, is the main goal of so-called 'fast tracks' or high potential programmes.

> 'We know that executives learn best from on-the-job experiences, so it is key to have a development plan in place for top key talent and to execute the plan effectively.'
>
> *Sherry H Stuckey, Glaxo-Wellcome*  **99**

As the number of desirable experiences has increased, the opportunities for job movement have often reduced with slower growth and leaner structures. So the emphasis has switched from maximum speed of movement and job variety to *adequate breadth and high challenge* work experience.

Many organisations find the notion of planned job experience difficult to sell to line managers, and sometimes employees may be wary of it. Lateral moves are therefore usually difficult to achieve and are unlikely to take place without some central encouragement and broking. Succession planning or something very like it is the only systematic process we see which overtly agrees and engineers such cross-boundary moves.

The positive levers for cross-boundary moves are:

- convincing line managers they will gain good staff as well as lose the ones they have now — the 'fair trade' principle

- supporting staff who are willing to make unusual moves, by not exposing them to unreasonable risk, and ensuring some career gain.

Development schemes can also formalise experience of a range of jobs. These are common for trainees, and also for potential managers. Job rotation and secondments are additional devices for giving broader experience. Some of these may be delivered by 'reserving' some particular posts as 'developmental'. This is still quite common at junior levels but rare at middle management and above.

It is important that individuals understand how training fits in with broader development. Succession planning is still sometimes used to identify, approve and schedule major training investment in individuals (*eg* international business school programmes).

If individuals are to feel committed to the kind of development the organisation has in mind for them, they need some mechanism for interacting with the succession planning process, hence our final critical link: that between succession planning and the individual.

## 5.4 Succession and the individual

There are a number of reasons why it is now vital to have very strong and clear links between individual employees and the succession planning process. Briefly these are:

- People make their own career decisions. Successful people have arguably always managed their own careers and will turn down jobs they are offered which they do not want. It is dysfunctional for organisations to plan career paths for individuals without checking their own thoughts on this matter.

- The timing of job moves is a tactical one for organisations, but also for individuals. An individual may be offered a job, but it is normally a family unit which decides whether to take it. Individuals' views on mobility depend on their career stage, family circumstances, and where you are asking them to move to. Dual career couples face particular challenges in relocating and are becoming the norm among managerial and professional groups. It is especially crucial for international companies to be open with individuals about these issues.

- Knowing that your employer is paying serious attention to your future career is flattering and adds significantly to the positive aspects of your psychological contract. If they plan for you, they must value you. But if they plan for you and you do not know they are doing this, that positive gain has been wasted. Many are the companies who have confessed to losing high potential people who were never told that they featured on succession plans and that exciting options were there for them.

- Succession planning can be seen as an unpleasantly elitist activity. *'Normal people have to manage their own careers, special people get theirs done for them.'* Such a stark difference falls foul of current corporate values and socially acceptable norms. Sitting succession within a strong self-development culture and using processes for 'special people' which include the need for them to actively manage their own careers and development, blurs the divide and reduces some of the negative elitism of the old way of doing things.

Linking the individual to succession planning is something organisations see as problematic. The main concern they voice is the problem of 'seeming to give promises' which they cannot necessarily deliver. One suspects, however, that the real concern is that they will have to have conversations with people about their careers which executives would sometimes sooner avoid.

'Succession and Development Plans are useless unless they are aligned with the interests and aspirations of the individual concerned. Sharing the information is often ignored or avoided for fear of "exciting expectations". In most cases, however, individuals underestimate their potential. They need support and encouragement to believe they can grow further.'

*Tony Ryan, BBC* **99**

The many organisations which have gone down the road of opening up the succession planning process tend to agree that it is not as difficult as they thought to talk to individuals about such plans. Indeed there are enormous gains to be made for the company through having more realistic plans and motivating high potential people by telling them they are highly valued.

'The worst thing you can do is fail to advise someone that they are part of the "grand plan" and, as a result, lose them.'

*Keith Brown, HSBC* **99**

The three critical processes required are:

- open information for *all* staff on how the succession planning process works and how it links with other HR systems (*eg* appraisal, job filling)

- input from every individual considered by the process on their plans, aspirations and constraints. This can be part of the appraisal process but is often better done separately. It may be done by their boss or boss's boss but a parallel discussion with HR can also be helpful. In organisations where personal development plans (PDPs) have taken root, some form of PDP may be the input the individual sends to the succession planning process.

- feedback to every individual considered by the process on how the organisation sees their potential, the kinds of job moves which the organisation might see as suitable and development actions suggested. Again, this is often done through the line but may also involve HR, functional heads or chairs of succession committees.

These dialogues with the individual should be serious conversations, not quick informal chats in corridors. The individual needs to be very clear about the purpose of the conversation and where it fits within the succession planning process. They also need to be told what will happen to the information they give and be able to request that some of the things they say be treated in confidence. This is especially important in succession planning as the information is shared between very senior and influential people in the business. It is also discussed when the individual is not present and so they need to trust that their views will not be misrepresented.

A philosophy of considering each person very much as an individual may also help to address some of the diversity issues raised in Section 4.1. Trying to see the organisation from the individual's point of view may help executives understand why certain groups do not see themselves as having potential, or do not see senior roles as attractive.

> We have encouraged people to own their careers and to manage their plans and activities accordingly. In return, people expect to have answers to key questions such as 'how do I plan, where do I search for opportunities, and what do I need to be successful?'
>
> *Les Slaytor, Rolls-Royce plc* 99

The senior person in HR taking responsibility for facilitating the succession process is often crucial in checking and challenging the line's view of what an individual may want, and establishing a good level of trust among individuals in the integrity of the succession planning process.

# 6. Supporting and Embedding Succession

So far we have been describing succession planning and where it fits into the business. We have already learned that it requires a collective, disciplined approach — not something managers usually apply spontaneously to human resource management. In this chapter we look at some of the practical issues in supporting the line in carrying out succession planning and sustaining the disciplines required.

## 6.1 The role of HR

Managers will not voluntarily commit time to succession planning if not helped to do so by a facilitating function. This is usually HR, but sometimes a separate function reporting direct to the Chief Executive.

The HR support is there to make sure the process happens, to manage the flow of information, to act as an impartial adviser, and to liase with individuals. In multi-layer or devolved succession processes, the HR function needs to co-ordinate across the boundaries, and help resolve any conflicts.

The role of HR in succession planning requires credibility, skill and real time. It is too often over-delegated or seen as a 'hobby' in an already busy job.

The general role of the HR function in succession planning can best be described as that of facilitator, but this term does not really do justice to the range of activities HR carries out. A project conducted by the Careers Research Forum identified a number of

**Figure 6.1: The role of HR in succession planning**

> **Process designer:** Advising on how information should be collected and collated. Framing agendas and questions.
>
> **Process manager/facilitator:** Direct personal involvement in making sure meetings happen and, on occasion, acting as 'referee' in ensuring the discussion is wide ranging and objective.
>
> **Goad and conscience:** Looking further to the future; asking 'seriously difficult' questions; highlighting problems that executives may prefer not to see.
>
> **Direct personal intervention as broker:** Knowing people well enough to be able to suggest successors, candidates for vacancies;,development opportunities for individuals and influencing executives to take these suggestions on board.
>
> **Counsellor:** Trusted to help executives talk through their issues and to help individuals work out their career directions.
>
> **Information support:** Maintaining quality information which delivers a direct service when internal candidate search is required, or more general questions are asked.

*Source: Hirsh, 1998*

different ways in which HR facilitates the process, as shown in Fig 6.1.

Organisations resource this range of roles in varied ways. For example, the information support role is often a more junior one. A number of the roles may be conducted both by local personnel and at the corporate centre. A common weakness is to fail to assign serious responsibility for succession planning to someone within the business streams of a devolved business. The 'goad' and 'broker' roles, both at corporate and business stream levels, require one or more people who can operate at the most senior level and who have credibility within the business and really know the key people, including younger high potential staff. Junior people cannot really do this. Senior people need to get involved in detail as well as in strategy.

## 6.2 The role of the CEO

The CEO always needs to support strategic HR processes, but with succession this need is heightened. Succession is not a process the CEO agrees to and then other people get on with. Succession is in many ways their own process. They have to lead it and get involved in a very hands-on way.

The Institute for Employment Studies

Recent trends in succession planning towards a more collective approach and stronger links with business and HR strategy, place the CEO in an even more pivotal role in the process than in the past. If the CEO does not support cross-unit moves they will not happen, as directors will then revert to hanging onto their best people.

CEOs with a reputation for positive people leadership have often been strong champions of a developmental approach to succession planning. Jack Welch at General Electric is a legendary example of someone taking a personal interest in young high potential managers.

HR people facilitating a succession planning process and the actions which stem from it, need to know their CEO will back them if executives don't supply information, or fail to abide by agreed actions.

All this demands somewhat selfless as well as energetic CEOs. Top people don't always like to think about succession. Kets de Vries (1988) sees the personal desire to stay in charge as the 'dark side' of succession. Sonnenfeld and Ward (1995) classify CEOs into different personal types: monarchs, generals, ambassadors and governors. Of these the first two do not wish to leave office at all, and will tend to see successors as enemies.

## 6.3  Supporting devolved succession planning

Many organisations aspire to implement what we have been calling a 'devolved' approach to succession planning. In this model the corporate centre takes direct responsibility for the very top of the organisation and relatively small numbers of high potential staff, but business divisions and sometimes functions will extend the process downwards.

Such a devolved approach raises some difficult issues as regards support and resourcing. They include:

- the need for the CEO to hold heads of divisions or functions responsible for conducting the succession planning process seriously. One way of achieving this is for the CEO to challenge directly the succession plans of those below and for this challenge process to run right down the line. This requires a culture of strong management accountability and high trust.

- the ability to get cross-boundary moves to happen for high potential staff in early or mid-career. Some organisations do this by having a clear high potential development scheme which treats longer term successors overtly as a corporate resource (BP Amoco does this, as do Merrill and Mobil, see Corporate Leadership Council, 1997). Other corporate centres do not intervene so visibly in the career management of younger high potential people, but may perform a more informal broking role.

- whether a devolved approach takes on board the desire to deliver proactive development for much larger populations of professional and managerial staff who are not necessarily defined as 'high potential'. Organisations like United Biscuits have adopted the philosophy of extending to much of their management population the same attention to development that they give to the most senior managers.

- at divisional, site, or functional level, the HR support for succession is likely to be bolted onto a generalist Personnel Manager post or a broad Employee Development/ Management Development role. There is a tendency for succession planning to be pushed down the priority order by other more urgent (although perhaps less important) tasks. It is also often delegated to someone of too low a level in the HR function to have the necessary dialogue with senior managers. Even if part of a wider job at local level, succession planning needs to be seen as a high priority task, not an occasional hobby, and one which rests with a person of considerable clout and credibility in the business.

## 6.4 Managing the data

Succession management can be seen as centred around information. Different kinds of information are involved:

- information about people and posts
- hard information (facts) and much soft information (assessments and opinions)
- information about specific individuals and information on aggregates (manpower planning and skill needs).

There are clearly benefits to holding some of the information used in succession planning in computerised form.

Data on individual employees is a mixture of hard and soft data. Well coded personal details and job history are extremely valuable for candidate search. Training records need not be elaborate for the purpose of a succession database. Likewise, holding large volumes of assessment data can be counterproductive. Summary information can be much more useful.

Employees should know what information is being held about them and, preferably, have a chance to check the accuracy of factual information and how their own preferences and aspirations are being summarised. As the phased implementation of the 1998 Data Protection Act comes into force, organisations need to be increasingly transparent about the data they hold (whether on computer or not) and how it will be used.

Databases on posts are usually less well developed than those on people. With frequent changes in organisation structure, it is worth concentrating on the few items of information about posts which are of most value: current post holder, level, function, and particular skill needs. This data is critical if you are searching for opportunities for developmental job movement. Information on groups of posts also becomes very important for individuals who are managing their own careers and wish to understand what options there are and what skills they need.

Computer systems have often not been designed with career management in mind. If you are re-examining the need for computerised information for career management, there are a number of factors to consider:

- Career history, intelligent job coding, and the ability to obtain aggregate data should be essentials.
- Post records are valuable and a system needs to link these with people records.
- Standard personnel systems hold very little assessment data — but opinions differ on the wisdom of holding more.
- Job and skill profiling systems promise much, but very few companies have managed to sustain their use for significant populations (*ie* a few hundred different jobs) over several years.
- There is a trade off between complexity and accuracy. Systems cannot be trusted in candidate search if they are not very accurate. So it is better to hold limited information and hold it well than to hold too much. Updating is the critical constraint, and should influence design and implementation.
- Access to information and the need for flexibility in reports will also influence information system design.

A centralised separate information system is often used for corporate succession purposes (usually top layer and fast track). Such systems still need links with personnel records for updating. The most successful seem to be home-grown databases which hold exactly what the company needs, built on the back of general purpose database software. Some organisations use proprietary software although this usually needs to be tailored to hold what the organisation wants.

In a more devolved process where a larger population may be involved, it helps enormously to hold the data in similar format on integrated systems or on the main personnel record system.

The Institute for Employment Studies

# 7. Is Succession Planning Meeting the Challenge?

In this final chapter we summarise some of the ways in which succession planning has adapted to the challenges raised at the beginning of the report. We also look at how we might judge its effectiveness, and why organisations still find value in planning for posts and people.

We finish with some thoughts on where best to start in an organisation which does not currently have a succession planning process, and the final section (Chapter 8) of the report summarises some 'practical tips' from the report as a whole.

## 7.1 Adaptations to the succession planning process

At the beginning of this report we suggested that 'traditional' succession planning needs to rise to the challenge of a changing environment if it is to be of practical value to organisations.

Certainly there is evidence that major UK employers are putting more rather than less effort into the pro-active career development of senior and high potential staff (Guest 1996; Hirsh and Jackson, 1996; Herriot and Pemberton, 1995). Thomson (1997) found that in a sample of over 500 medium sized organisations, 60 per cent had some form of succession planning, although this was often informal.

We hope that this account of succession planning, based as it is on emergent good practice, shows that the old model of names in boxes is evolving into 'new style' succession planning: something

**Figure 7.1: Key features of 'new style' succession planning**

- Strong emphasis on using succession planning as a process for pro-actively developing 'talent', and therefore an emphasis on engineering developmental work experiences.

- Planning for 'pools' of jobs where possible not just for individual posts.

- A more devolved model with only very senior roles and small 'high potential' populations planned for at the corporate centre.

- Acceptance of the need for a more diverse senior management group, with functional strength as well as general management skills.

- Consideration of future skill needs as well as current skills (linked to but not restricted to competence frameworks).

- More objective information on the performance, skills and potential of individuals *ie* a meritocratic philosophy.

- A collective management process for identifying successors and taking responsibility for their development.

- More involvement of the individual and a gradual shift towards a more open approach. This includes adapting succession to take account of increasingly open internal job advertising.

- Less emphasis on 'the plan' but more on the dialogue and the valuable database which is built through the process and can be used in a variety of ways (*eg* candidate search, during reorganisations *etc*.)

- Line ownership, often led by the CEO, with active facilitation and support from HR.

*Source: IES*

much more flexible, realistic and dynamic. It is an attempt to recognise the legitimate criticisms (summarised earlier in Figure 2.2) while also facing up to the necessity to be proactive in the development of successors.

Some of the key features of the 'new style' model of succession planning are shown Figure 7.1.

'Succession planning works more effectively when:

- it enables managers to have focussed discussions about the development needs of its talent pool

- there are specific and agreed criteria for judging performance which are used in the discussions. Managers demonstrate individuals' performance against these criteria and this is supplemented or challenged by colleagues until a joint view is achieved.

- the headlines from this process are fed back to the individual to enable them to plan their learning goals.'

*Sue Purves, AstraZeneca*                                            **99**

## 7.2 New ways of thinking about succession planning

As well as evolution in how organisations *do* succession planning, there are parallel changes which need to take place in the way we *think* about succession.

In the '60s and '70s succession was about *planning* and also about *how the organisation was going to fill key jobs.*

In thinking about succession today, some of the key ideas seem to be: *development, dialogue, improving information,* and *responding to change.* Succession is seen both as a *management process* and as *supportive of individuals managing their own careers.*

'Having a clear, achievable plan for succession to key senior positions remains important, but should not obscure the more important goal which is to develop a sustainable pipeline of talent to support and deliver the organisation's ambitions over time.'

*Stephen Dando, Guinness Limited*                           **99**

The *process* for succession planning is seen as having value as well as its practical outcomes. It is a process which makes senior managers more aware of people issues and more engaged in employee development. It also increases their own skills in making judgements about people. It is therefore a *learning* process for those involved in doing it.

# 7.3 Evidence of effectiveness

Just because most large employers think they should be doing succession planning, does that mean it adds real value?

Given the multiple purposes of succession planning outlined in Chapter 2, we might put forward a number of different criteria for judging its success. The balance between these will vary according to which purposes are held to be most important. Hirsh (1998) found that the purposes of audit and development were held to be of more importance than job filling.

> 'Succession planning is too often a meaningless HR driven paper exercise. The vital question is what is different as a result; what actions does it lead to that, in themselves, impact on the organisation's short- and long-term performance?'
>
> *Nick Holley, M&G Ltd (Prudential)*                                    **99**

Some measures of effectiveness might be:

**Do jobs get filled by identified successors?** Organisations tend not to expect jobs to be always filled by their identified successors, but do expect successors to get onto the shortlist in the majority of cases. If jobs never get filled by identified successors, some hard questions should be asked.

**Is the job filling process faster/better?** Does the succession process help those filling jobs to identify suitable candidates of good quality? This can come from improved candidate search but also from an improvement over time in the quality of candidates.

**Is the data produced through succession planning of value?** Is the database trawled when vacancies come up? Does this generate good candidates who would otherwise have been overlooked? Is succession data used in times of change (*eg* mergers, restructuring)?

**Is the 'pipeline' improving?** We can, and should, measure whether planned development is followed up. We can, more subjectively, assess whether skills identified as in short supply improve over a period of time. It is not difficult to identify jobs which are hard to fill and track the changes in these jobs types over time.

**Are cross-boundary moves taking place?** A concrete intention is often to ensure that high potential people get experience across functional or business unit boundaries. Cross-boundary moves should be tracked as a way of seeing if this is delivered.

**What happens to hi-pos?** It seems only common-sense to track individuals identified as 'high potential' to see where they go and how well they perform. This is rarely done, but should be!

**Retention and motivation.** Two of the most important drivers for active succession planning are retention and motivation of key staff. These are rarely tracked at all, and quite difficult to ascribe to the succession process, or lack of it. However, surveys of staff could at least be used to identify levels of satisfaction with specific aspects of succession (*eg* 'the business invests in its best people').

We would like to be able to assess whether succession planning leads to more profitable organisations (in the private sector) or more effective ones (in the public sector). Friedman (1986) attempted to look at this in the US. He found a number of succession factors positively related to financial corporate performance: the time and resources spent on succession issues; good quality information; the credibility of the HR champion; and the direct involvement of the CEO. It was not the formality of the process which seemed to make a difference but the seriousness with which top management addressed succession issues. This finding is highly consistent with the philosophy behind current trends (see Section 7.1).

A survey conducted among 38 major UK employers who were members of the Careers Research Forum (Hirsh, 1998) found that:

- forty-five per cent had been doing formal succession planning for more than five years, 31 per cent had started in the last five years and 24 per cent were not doing it at all

- those with a formal process were likely (70 per cent) to have regular discussion of succession issues by the Board or Executive Committee (compared with 33 per cent of those without a formal process)

- those who had a formal succession planning process for over five years were more satisfied with their ability to fill senior positions; more likely to report proactive development of high potential people; proactive moves for senior managers and proactive moves for high potential people. They were also more likely to feel they had good information on potential internal candidates, and to discuss possible job moves with individuals.

● perhaps surprisingly, organisations conducting succession planning were more likely to advocate self-managed careers and to advertise senior vacancies internally. So they seemed to be using a 'both and' model of career development, *ie* expecting both the employing organisation and the individual to be active in career development.

Chambers *et al.* (1998) link the effectiveness of succession management with what they call 'superior employee value propositions.' Their claim is that organisations which offer such superior propositions outperform others in business terms because they have a 'stronger pull on talent'. Key elements of the proposition are freedom and autonomy; exciting business and job challenges; and career advancement and growth. Although succession planning does not deliver any of these of itself, it may be instrumental in ensuring that high potential people do get challenging jobs and attention is paid to their career advancement.

# 7.4 Factors influencing success or failure

Many organisations always seem 'just about to' implement a succession process. They never quite get round to it, or start something up only to have it lapse very quickly. This was the commonest reason for not doing succession planning in the CRF study referred to above (Hirsh, 1998).

Some of the underpinning factors for sustaining effective succession planning include:

● whether the business takes a corporate long-term view of itself, and therefore of its management assets

● whether the line, and especially the CEO, take the performance and development of people seriously, as Chambers *et al.* (1998) say: '*Companies must insist that their line managers are accountable for talent*'

● whether the senior team can work together on difficult issues and find a language in which to discuss the value and potential of individuals to the business

- whether the HR function is competent, well organised (especially in data management) and can hold its own in a discussion of key people and positions with the executive team
- whether enough HR resource of suitable quality is devoted to facilitating the succession planning process.

A lack of several of these factors is identified by Andrews and Munroe (1999) as accounting for their fairly pessimistic findings on the state of succession management practice in 40 UK organisations. Three particular weaknesses they identify are:

- lack of commitment from the top
- lack of systematic information capture (and poor use of IT)
- minimal use of experiential learning, in particular of job moves.

# 7.5 So why look at 'successors'?

So, let's return to the debate for and against formal succession planning raised in Chapter 2. Why do so many major corporations insist on still conducting detailed succession planning when it has so many problems in an uncertain time?

In theory, a process which reviews management talent without looking at successors for particular types of post, should deliver many of the benefits of formal succession planning. The sad truth is that a broad brush approach doesn't seem to work. It seems to be that the process of considering successors in a fairly rigorous way against different jobs or types of job delivers three things other more general reviews can't deliver:

1. It highlights specific deficits in the management population and pipeline which more general reviews based on generic management skills tend to miss.
2. It simultaneously highlights individual development needs of possible successors.
3. It also provides a means for agreeing cross-boundary or unusual job moves/experiences for these individuals.

So it is the maddeningly specific nature of formal succession planning — the very thing which seems so inappropriate in a fast changing world — which seems to be its particular strength. Major employers haven't yet found a way of achieving this without looking at the real jobs and real people they have today, even if they know they will be different tomorrow.

> 'The outcome is improved planning for individuals and fast track focussed development. The summative plan gives an opportunity for the management team to audit their success in developing individuals and highlight areas for attention and external benchmarking.'
>
> *Sue Purves, AstraZeneca*                                                **99**

# 7.6 Challenges

This report has tried to demystify contemporary succession planning, but we should not pretend that the current mixture of evolving practices represents a solution to the dilemmas of succession planning. The process has to deal with some fundamental tensions which can't be solved, only managed. They include:

- the need to plan but the inevitability that specific plans for people and posts will need to be continuously reviewed and updated as circumstances change. So the planning process must not get too slow or bureaucratised.

- the need to make holistic judgements about people, but also to have an analytical understanding of what skills are of importance to the future business, and sound evidence for assessments. So skill or competence frameworks are helpful but not if used too mechanistically. Differences of opinion about people need to be argued out by using examples of what they have actually done at work.

- the need for the business to meet its own needs but also to take on board fully that people make their own decisions about their own careers. So individuals need to feed information into succession and get feedback from it.

- the need to build on existing corporate strengths but also to take on board the diverse range of key posts (not just general management) and to widen the kinds of people who enter the highest levels of corporate life. In particular, succession planning should be a driver for more women and ethnic minorities reaching the top. The relatively closed nature of succession planning can easily add to suspicion of unfairness (Guest and Mackenzie-Davey, 1996). Some American organisations have used succession as a lever for achieving a more diverse senior management population (*eg* Merrill, in Corporate Leadership

Council, 1997; and Avon, in Morris, 1997), but examples of this are rare in the UK.

- the necessity of devolving to divisional or functional levels much of the succession planning activity, but the need to insist on corporate quality standards and on treating talent as a corporate resource. If such devolved succession processes are to be sustained, they have to be given the same importance and level of support as the process run at the corporate centre for the most senior grades.

## 7.7 Where do you start?

Succession planning is a learning experience for all involved. Successful systems evolve over time and often need to adjust to the shifting structure of a large organisation.

'We evolved a process for one kind of organisation and, now the organisation has changed, to one with a larger number of smaller business units. We are building on our past experience but adjusting the process to the new organisation. Adjusting to major organisational change can mean running with a less sophisticated process for a while and then moving forward again.'

*Helen Bartolome, Post Office*

Succession planning needs professional support to flourish, but we also need to keep a balance between:

- addressing the **strategic issues** (*eg* resourcing strategy, skill needs) and the **individual issues** (*ie* particular people and posts)
- processes which **generate information** (especially assessment processes, database development) and processes which lead to **action** (*ie* formulating intentions and using plans in job filling and development).

A balanced strategy seems to move around these activities. As more information is available, so it is put to use. Using information demands higher quality inputs, so background information or assessment issues are then addressed. Background information activities have a key role, but should not be allowed to get out of hand.

Succession planning most often starts near the top of the organisation with a limited population of jobs and then may grow into the devolved model with different groups of jobs and people being planned for at different locations in the organisation. Sometimes it is a function which takes the lead. Finance Directors often initiate succession planning for their own function, partly because of the need to plan early training, but also because no-one else seems to take responsibility for this group. If one function pilots an approach, others may then take it on board.

So succession processes should not be over-designed at the beginning. The Board will enjoy getting a detailed paper from HR, which they will accept — and then do nothing about!

The HR function needs to involve the senior team in talking through the purposes of succession planning (which they are often unclear about) and in setting down some shared principles and a skeleton process. They then need to try this process out and refine it from there.

# 8. Practical Tips

1. Be clear about the scope of jobs you are trying to cover initially. Start with a scale you can manage. Remember you need to look at short- and longer-term successors for these posts as well as current post holders, so the population of people is always considerably larger than the population of posts.

2. Where possible, group jobs together so that successors can be identified for the collection of jobs, not each job separately. Some jobs, however, will still need to be planned for individually, especially those which are truly critical ones.

3. Set a short list of questions which you want a succession review to cover. Get each major part of the business to conduct their own review. Discuss it with HR and possibly the CEO before the heads of the businesses (usually at Board level) come together to conduct an overall review. Consider whether the heads of functions should also review each main function across business units in the same way.

4. Use collective review meeting(s) to challenge the first round plans, identify key issues (*eg* areas of shortage or changing skill needs) and developmental actions for individuals, especially cross-boundary job moves. Record planned actions, and at subsequent meetings review progress on these actions. Be clear who is accountable for them.

5. Relate succession to existing frameworks for technical and generic competencies, but do not restrict the skills discussed to those on the generic competence list. Ask whether successors support the values of the organisation as well as having the required skills. Check that women and ethnic minorities are not overlooked in the succession planning process.

6. Consider how jobs are going to be affected in terms of numbers and skills over the next few years by anticipated business changes. Build this into the numbers and skills of successors you identify.

7.  Ensure that when a job vacancy arises, the succession plans and database are examined, to influence the candidate pool and to see whether this vacancy is a critical one to use for a developmental job move.

8.  Make sure all staff are told clearly how the succession planning process works. Explain where it fits with other HR processes and where the data comes from which will inform succession judgements. Those discussed in the process should have an opportunity to make an input via a PDP or statement about their aspirations and preferences. They should also receive feedback on how their potential is viewed by the organisation and for what kinds of jobs they might be considered.

9.  Set up a simple database of information, at least on the post holders and successors, as soon as you can. Use a package you already have and use your prototype to learn what information you really need to keep. Remember the need to update continuously. Try coding key items of information. Do this before investing time and money in purchasing or developing a sophisticated system.

10. Use a senior HR person with credibility at the highest levels in the business to co-ordinate the succession process with support for them on information gathering and analysis. Involve the CEO and Directors from the start. Do it with them not for them.

11. If there is to be a devolved aspect of succession planning covering lower job levels within divisions, locations or functions, make sure it is properly resourced and not just tacked onto an existing busy job.

12. Don't over-design the process. Expect the senior team to take a simple framework and evolve it to meet their business needs. Help them to see it as a collective learning experience. Get them to reflect collectively and individually on how they feel the process is working, especially how well they are sharing information and making judgements about people.

13. Don't let the process lapse when the key players change jobs — doing something simple and acting on it for several years is much more effective then doing something ambitious for only a year or so.

# Appendix: Case Examples from Published Studies

**Please note**: Succession processes evolve continuously. Examples here are drawn from fairly recent literature, but several of the organisations have gone through major organisational change (*eg* mergers) in the last couple of years and most will have continued to adapt their succession planning processes to their ever-changing needs.

## Key learning points:

### IRS (1997)

| | |
|---|---|
| **Glaxo-Wellcome** | Retention of talent is a key driver for succession planning. |
| | High potential staff are given developmental postings. |
| | International moves are centrally co-ordinated. |

| | |
|---|---|
| **Halifax** | Skill deployment across the organisation is a key driver, and therefore broadening experience is an outcome sought. |
| | A network of committees is used. |
| | Competence based processes, with a specific skill framework for the top layer of the organisation. |
| | Succession planning sits within a self-development culture. |
| | All staff are informed about the nature of the process. |

**Hirsh (1998)**

| | |
|---|---|
| **Prudential** | Succession in a devolved business is about identifying key issues and challenging the plans of business divisions. |
| | Corporate succession pitched at short- and longer-term ('pipeline') successors for the top jobs. |
| | CEO and HR Director personally involved. They discuss each business with the Head and HR Director of that business. |
| | Functions are reviewed across the group. |
| | HR helps to broker moves for those in the 'pipeline' for senior roles. |
| | Each business can adapt the review approach to suit its needs. |
| **Post Office** | Corporate centre works closely with major business divisions. |
| | Corporate process covers the most senior jobs (Executive Committees and MDs of business units) but also takes an interest in the wider population of managers which are the responsibility of the business units. |
| | Moving towards planning for 'job families' (broad functions) and types of job role. |
| | A regional process has been used to stimulate cross-business and cross-functional moves for those well below the top levels. |
| | Integrated information is important to effective succession planning. |
| **BP** | Succession formally for the 'group leadership' and most of these looked at as 'pools' not individual posts. |
| | Functions looked at across the businesses. |
| | Interlinked committees are used for the succession planning process. |
| | Corporate high potential scheme (IPD scheme) identifies people in earlier career. Their development is linked to the succession process. |
| | PDP is part of the input to succession process and there should also be feedback from succession planning to the individual. Line manager has a key role in mediating between the organisation and the individual. |
| | Home-grown succession database, evolved and tailored over several years to meet business needs. |

The Institute for Employment Studies

| **Cabinet Office** for the Civil Service | Central succession plans for top levels only, although departments and agencies should be looking lower down. A larger group (the Senior Civil Service) is of corporate interest. |
| --- | --- |
| | Succession fed by dialogue between the Cabinet Office and Permanent Secretaries of each Department. |
| | Centre acts in brokering role for high potential people to move across Departments and Agencies. |
| | Process is still fairly closed but getting gradually more open to individuals. |

| **Zeneca** | Central HR works closely with CEOs of main businesses. |
| --- | --- |
| | Heads of major functions carry out a parallel review. |
| | Also more local reviews of people at rather lower levels in the business. |
| | Looks at successors but also at wider issues (*eg* retention). |
| | Strong emphasis on line accountability for succession and development. |

# Bibliography

Andrews, Munroe (1999), *Best Practice Succession and Resourcing: Survey Results*, AM Ltd

Arnold J (1997), *Managing Careers into the 21st Century*, London: Paul Chapman Publishing Ltd

Arnold J (1998), 'Post–Modern Career Management', *Human Resources*, Jan/Feb

Chambers E, Foulon M, *et al.* (1998), 'The War for Talent', *McKinsey Quarterly*

Corporate Leadership Council (1997), *The Next Generation: Accelerating the Development of Rising Leader*, Washington DC: The Advisory Board Company

Corporate Leadership Council (1998), *Forced Outside: Leadership Talent Sourcing and Retention*, Washington DC: The Advisory Board Company

Eastman L J (1995), *Succession Planning. Centre for Creative Leadership*, Greensboro, North Carolina

Fletcher C (1999), 'The implications of research on gender differences in self-assessment and 360 degree appraisal', *Human Resource Management Journal*, Vol. 9, No. 1

Friedman S D (1986), 'Succession Systems in Large Corporations: Characteristics and Correlates of Performance', *Human Resource Management*, Vol. 25(2), pp. 191–213

Gratton L, Syrett M (1990), 'Heirs Apparent: Succession Strategies for the Future', *Personnel Management*, January

Guest D, Mackenzie-Davey K (1996), 'Don't Write Off the Traditional Career', *People Management*, February

Hall D T (1986), 'Dilemmas in Linking Succession Planning to Individual Executive Learning', *Human Resource Management*, Vol. 25(2), pp. 235–265

Herriot P (1992), *The Career Management Challenge: Balancing Individual and Organisational Needs*, Sage

Herriot P, Pemberton C (1995), *New Deals: The Revolution in Management Careers*, John Wiley & Sons

Hirsh W (1990), *Succession Planning: Current Practice and Future Issues*, IMS Report 184, Brighton: Institute of Manpower Studies (now Institute for Employment Studies)

Hirsh W, Jackson C (1996), *Strategies for Career Development: Promise, Practice and Pretence*, IES Report 305, Brighton: Institute for Employment Studies

Hirsh W, Reilly P (1998), 'Skills planning', *People Management*, July, pp. 38-41

Hirsh W (1998), *Planning for succession: from forms to content?* Careers Research Forum (available on www.crforum.co.uk)

Hirsh W, Pollard E, Tamkin P (2000), *Free, Fair and Efficient? Open Internal Job Advertising*, IES Report 371

Holbeche L (1998), *High Flyers and Succession Planning in Changing Organisations*, Horsham: Roffey Park

IRS (1997), 'Planning Succession in a Climate of Organisational Change', *IRS Employee Development Bulletin*, No. 96, December

Kets de Fries M F R (1998), 'The Dark Side of CEO Succession', *Harvard Business Review*, Vol. 88(1), pp. 56-60

Liebman M (1996), 'Succession Management: The Next Generation of Succession Planning', *Human Resource Planning*, Vol. 19(3), pp. 16-29

Mayo A (1991), *Managing Careers: Strategies for Organizations*, London: Institute of Personnel Management

Morris B (1997), 'If Women Ran the World, It Would Look a Lot Like Avon', *Fortune*, Vol. 136(2), pp. 74–79

Peterson R B (1985), 'Latest Trends in Succession Planning', *Personnel*, August, pp. 47-54

Santora J, Sarros J C (1996), 'Does Power Determine Who Selects the Successor?', *Academy of Management Executive*, Vol. 10(4), pp. 107–108

Sarch Y (1993), 'Nothing Succeeds Like Succession Planning', *Human Resources*, Spring, pp. 90–94

Schall E (1997), 'Public Sector Succession: A Strategic Approach to Sustaining Innovation', *Public Administrations Review*, Vol. 57(1), pp. 4–10

Sonnenfeld J A, Ward A (1995), 'Being successful at succession', *Directors and Boards*, Vol. 19(4), pp. 17-21

Thomson A, Storey S, Mabey C, *et al.* (1997), *A Portrait of Management Development*, Institute of Management/Open University Business School

Tichy N (1996), 'Simultaneous Transformation and CEO Succession: Key to Global Competitiveness', *Organizational Dynamics*, Summer

Viney C, Adamson S, Doherty N (1997), 'Paradoxes of Fast Track Career Management', *Personnel Review*, Vol. 26(3), pp. 174–186

Wallum P (1993), 'A Broader View of Succession Planning', *Personnel Management*, September

White M C, Smith M, Barnett T (1997), 'CEO Succession: Overcoming Forces of Inertia', *Human Relations*, Vol. 50(7), pp. 805–827